Music FUNdamentals

44 Games That Teach Melodic and Rhythmic Concepts

D. Brian Weese

Editor: Jeanette Morgan
Cover Design and Illustrations: Patti Jeffers

© 2010 Heritage Music Press, a division of The Lorenz Corporation, and its licensors.

Heritage Music Press
A Lorenz Company
P.O. Box 802
Dayton, Ohio 45401
www.lorenz.com

HERITAGE MUSIC PRESS
Diverse Resources for *Your* Music Classroom
a Lorenz company • www.lorenz.com

Printed in the United States of America

ISBN: 978-1-4291-1750-0

Permission-to-Reproduce Notice
Permission to photocopy the student activities in this product is hereby granted to one teacher as part of the purchase price. This permission may not be transferred, sold, or given to any additional or subsequent user of this product. Thank you for respecting the copyright laws.

Contents

Game	Page Number
Note Name Words #1	3
Note Name Words #2	4
Note Name Words #3	5
Note Name Phrases #1	6
Note Name Phrases #2	7
Note Name Phrases #3	8
Reading Solfège #1	9
Reading Solfège #2	10
Reading Solfège #3	11
Melodic Direction #1	12
Melodic Direction #2	13
Melodic Direction #3	14
Going Up! Going Down! #1	15
Going Up! Going Down! #2	16
Going Up! Going Down! #3	17
Melody Fragments #1	18
Melody Fragments #2	20
Melody Fragments #3	22
Picture Rhythms #1	24
Picture Rhythms #2	25
Picture Rhythms #3	26
Rhythm Math #1	27
Rhythm Math #2	28
Rhythm Math #3	29
Case of the Missing Notes #1	30
Case of the Missing Notes #2	31
Case of the Missing Notes #3	32
Case of the Missing Notes #4	33
Case of the Missing Notes #5	34
Rhythm Logic #1	35
Rhythm Logic #2	36
Rhythm Logic #3	37
Mystery Rhythms #1	38
Mystery Rhythms #2	39
Mystery Rhythms #3	40
Transforming Rhythms #1	41
Transforming Rhythms #2	42
Transforming Rhythms #3	43
Meter Matching #1	44
Meter Matching #2	45
Meter Matching #3	46
Rhythigram #1	47
Rhythigram #2	48
Rhythigram #3	49
Answer Keys	50

Name _____ Date _____ Classroom Teacher _____

Note Name Words #1

Directions: Use the musical code below to fill in the blanks. Each word should spell an animal.

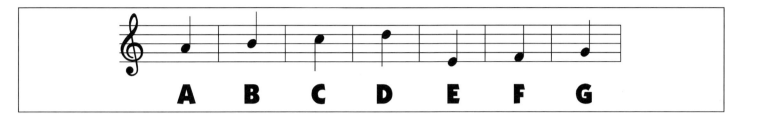

1.
__ O W

2.
R __ T

3.
__ O __

4.
__ __ T

5.
__ I R __

6.
__ __ R

7.
__ __ __

8.
P __ N __

9.
__ __ M __ L

10.
__ __ __ L __

© 2010 Heritage Music Press, a Lorenz company. All rights reserved.
This page may be reproduced for single-classroom use. This is a non-transferable license.

Name _____ Date _____ Classroom Teacher _____

Note Name Words #2

Directions: Use the musical code below to fill in the blanks. Each word should spell something you can eat or drink.

1.
   S O __ __

6.
   __ R __ P __

2.
   P __ __ R

7.
   __ __ __ O N

3.
   __ __ __ K

8.
   P __ __ __ H

4.
   __ __ __ N

9.
   __ __ __ __

5.
   __ __ __

10.
    __ __ __ __ L

© 2010 Heritage Music Press, a Lorenz company. All rights reserved.
This page may be reproduced for single-classroom use. This is a non-transferable license.

Name _____ Date _____ Classroom Teacher _____

Note Name Words #3

Directions: Use the musical code below to fill in the blanks. Each word should spell a toy or something that you can play with.

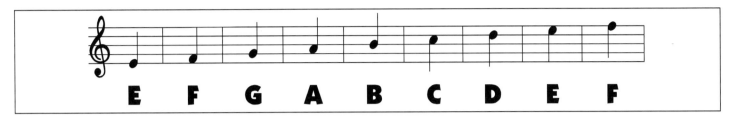

1.
_ _ R T

2.
_ _ _ R

3.
_ I _ _ _

4.
_ _ M _

5.
_ _ _ R _ S

6.
_ I _ Y _ L _

7.
_ _ R _ I _

8.
_ R I S _ _ _

9.
_ U _ L S

10.
_ _ N Y L N _

© 2010 Heritage Music Press, a Lorenz company. All rights reserved.
This page may be reproduced for single-classroom use. This is a non-transferable license.

Name _____   Date _____   Classroom Teacher _____

Note Name Phrases #1

Directions: Use the musical code below to fill in the blanks and reveal six wacky sentences.

1.
   _ __i__ _ir____ _o____ _ __st __t.

2.
   Th_ _mo___ _r_____ _ _l__k w___l_.

3.
   Th_ ___r__ _____r t_ _ ____l.

4.
   _n ___r _u__ _tt_n___ ___h_ _____my.

5.
   Th_ ___-h_____ i___ w_s ____t__.

6.
   Th_ ___s_ n__ to th_ r_____ ___t.

© 2010 Heritage Music Press, a Lorenz company. All rights reserved.
This page may be reproduced for single-classroom use. This is a non-transferable license.

Name _____ Date _____ Classroom Teacher _____

Note Name Phrases #2

Directions: Use the musical code below to fill in the blanks and reveal six wacky sentences.

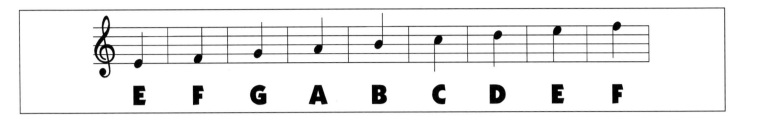

1.
   Th_ _o_ r_n _w_y _n_ _v___ __ptur_.

2.
   Th_ __m____ _____ w_nt to __n___.

3.
   Th_ _l___ __s____ ov_r th_ _ri___.

4.
   H_ _oun_ _ _____r in th_ __r____.

5.
   Th_y ___o___ _ m_ss___ with _ _____t.

6.
   Sh_ ___i___ to m_k_ ___n___ __m_.

© 2010 Heritage Music Press, a Lorenz company. All rights reserved.
This page may be reproduced for single-classroom use. This is a non-transferable license.

Name _____ Date _____ Classroom Teacher _____

Note Name Phrases #3

Directions: Musical notes can go above and below the musical staff to create higher and lower pitches. When notes go above, or below, the staff they use ledger lines to show you how high, or low, they are. Use the musical code below to fill in the blanks and reveal six wacky sentences.

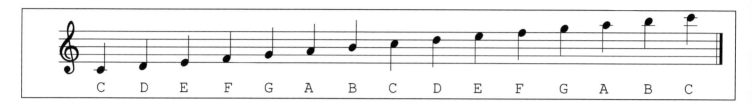

1.
   I ___r__ _ ___r___ in _l___r_.

2.
   _i__ _n_ __r_ __m_s _r_ r__lly _un.

3.
   Th_ _____ o_ th_ _r____ is _i_.

4.
   Th_ __t _r_wl__ un__r th_ _r___ t__l_.

5.
   Th_ _r___y m___ __k__ _ _r_n __k_.

6.
   Sh_ _t_ _n ___ _n_ sw__ _ur__ r.

© 2010 Heritage Music Press, a Lorenz company. All rights reserved.
This page may be reproduced for single-classroom use. This is a non-transferable license.

Name _____ Date _____ Classroom Teacher _____

Reading Solfège #1

Directions: Each measure below contains a melodic pattern using *mi*, *sol*, or *la* and has a letter under it. Use the *solfège* ladder at the right to help you determine where each pitch is located on the staff. Then, answer the jokes at the bottom of the page by matching the pattern below the blank with one of the patterns on the staff and writing the corresponding letter in the blank. Each letter will be used at least once. The first one has been done for you.

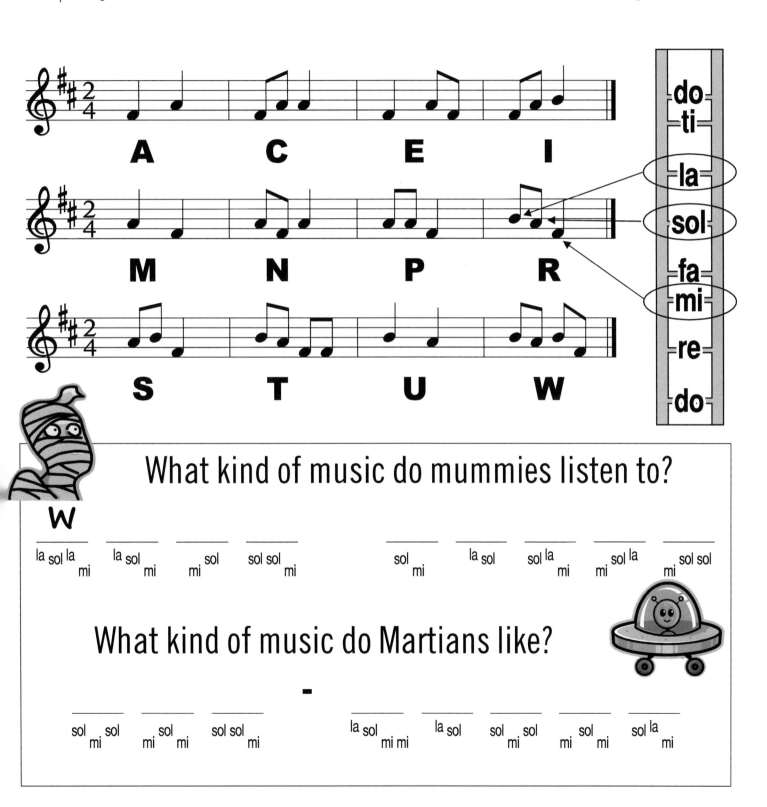

Name _____ Date _____ Classroom Teacher _____

Reading Solfège #2

Directions: Each measure below contains a melodic pattern using *mi*, *sol*, or *la* and has a letter under it. Use the *solfège* ladder at the right to help you determine where each pitch is located on the staff. Then, answer the joke at the bottom of the page by matching the pattern below the blank with one of the patterns on the staff and writing the corresponding letter in the blank. Each letter will be used at least once. The first one has been done for you.

Name _____ Date _____ Classroom Teacher _____

Reading Solfège #3

Directions: Each measure below contains a melodic pattern using *do*, *mi*, and *sol* and has a letter under it. Use the *solfège* ladder at the right to help you determine where each pitch is located on the staff. Then, answer the joke at the bottom of the page by matching the pattern below the blank with one of the patterns on the staff and writing the corresponding letter in the blank. Each letter will be used at least once. The first one has been done for you.

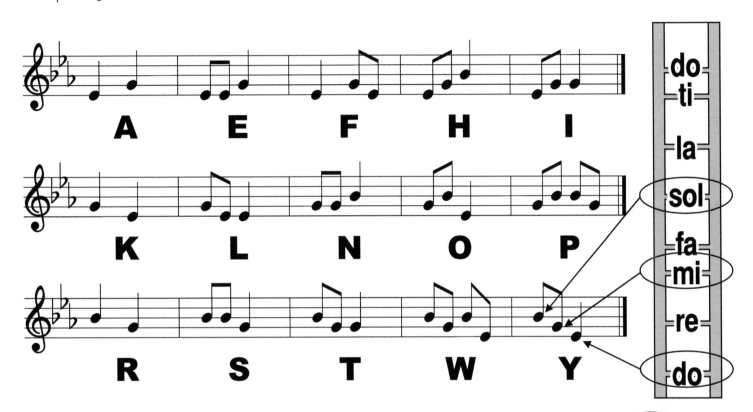

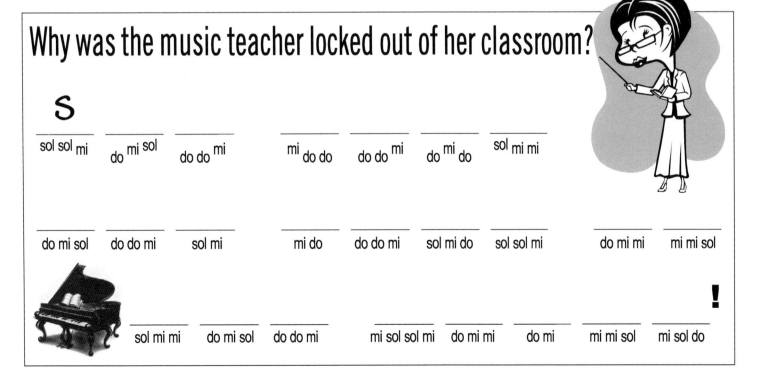

Name _____ Date _____ Classroom Teacher _____

Melodic Direction #1

Directions: The notes in a melody, or song, move up or down by steps, skips, leaps, and sometimes they repeat. Look at each box below and decide if the notes repeat or do not repeat. Circle the word "repeat" if the notes repeat and the words "no repeat" if they do not repeat. When you are done, answer the riddle below.

Notes that REPEAT — the note heads are on the same line or space.

Notes that do NOT REPEAT — the note heads are NOT on the same line or space.

What is a balloon's least favorite music?

____ ____ ____   ____ ____ ____ ____ ____

Write all the letters above the boxes where you circled the word "repeat," in the order they appear, to reveal the answer.

Name _____ Date _____ Classroom Teacher _____

Melodic Direction #2

Directions: The notes in a melody, or song, move up or down by steps, skips, leaps, and sometimes they repeat. Look at each box below and decide if the notes repeat, move by step, or move by skip. Circle the appropriate word. When you are done, answer the riddle below.

What food is essential for good music?

_____ _____ _____   _____ _____ _____ _____

Write all the letters above the boxes where you circled the word "repeat," in the order they appear, to reveal the answer.

© 2010 Heritage Music Press, a Lorenz company. All rights reserved.
This page may be reproduced for single-classroom use. This is a non-transferable license.

Name _____ Date _____ Classroom Teacher _____

Going Up! Going Down! #1

Directions: The "vertical distance" between two notes going up or down is called an interval. We use numbers to measure the distance—the bigger the number, the bigger the musical leap. To find the interval, count the number of lines and spaces between notes *including* the line or space of the two notes in the interval. Determine the interval between each set of notes. Write the direction (↑ or ↓) and the number of the interval on the top blank. Then, use the code below to write the corresponding letter beneath each interval. Each set of intervals should spell a common, everyday word. The first interval has been done for you.

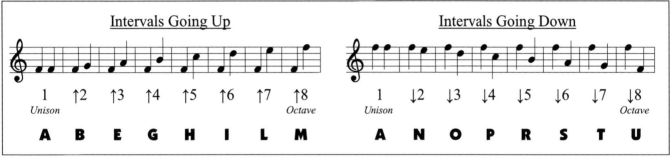

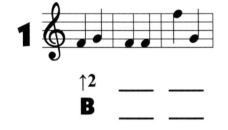

© 2010 Heritage Music Press, a Lorenz company. All rights reserved.
This page may be reproduced for single-classroom use. This is a non-transferable license.

Going Up! Going Down! #2

Directions: The "vertical distance" between two notes going up or down is called an interval. We use numbers to measure the distance—the bigger the number, the bigger the musical leap. To find the interval, count the number of lines and spaces between notes *including* the line or space of the two notes in the interval. Determine the interval between each set of notes. Write the direction (↑ or ↓) and the number of the interval on the top blank. Then, use the code below to write the corresponding letter beneath each interval. Each set of intervals should spell a common, everyday word. The first interval has been done for you.

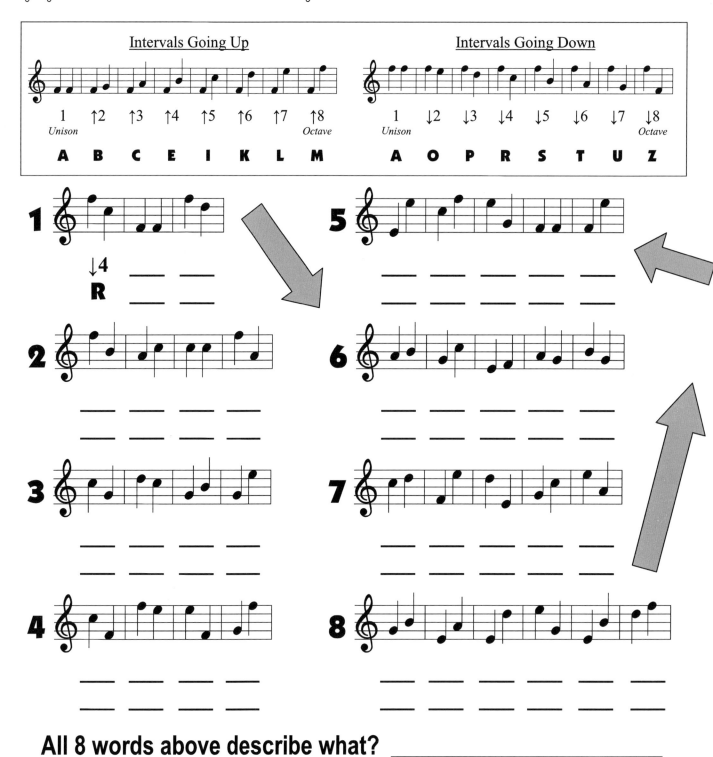

All 8 words above describe what? _____

Name _____ Date _____ Classroom Teacher _____

Going Up! Going Down! #3

Directions: The "vertical distance" between two notes going up or down is called an interval. We use numbers to measure the distance—the bigger the number, the bigger the musical leap. To find the interval, count the number of lines and spaces between notes *including* the line or space of the two notes in the interval. Determine the interval between each set of notes. Write the direction (↑ or ↓) and the number of the interval on the top blank. Then, use the code below to write the corresponding letter beneath each interval. Each set of intervals should spell a common, everyday word. The first interval has been done for you.

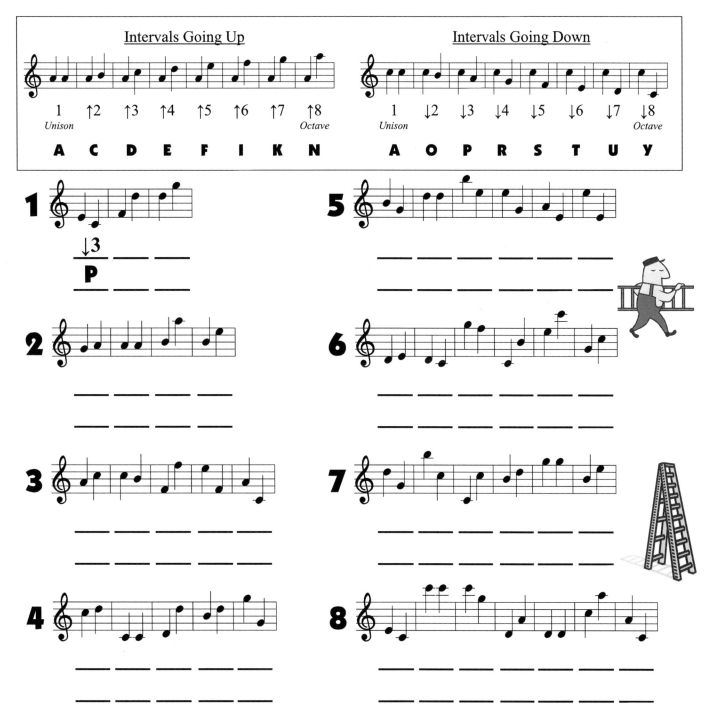

All 8 words above describe what? _____

Melody Fragments #1

Name _____ Date _____ Classroom Teacher _____

Directions: Below are 17 melody fragments from 5 different songs. Each fragment is either the first 2 beats of a measure or the last 2 beats of a measure. Match the melody fragments to the appropriate measures below. Neatly write the notes in the measure. One example has been done for you. Can you figure out the names of the songs? How many of these songs can you play on the xylophone or recorder?

Here are the names of the 5 songs:

Yankee Doodle   *Good King Wenceslas*   *Old MacDonald Had a Farm*   *Hot Cross Buns*   *Au Claire de la Lune*

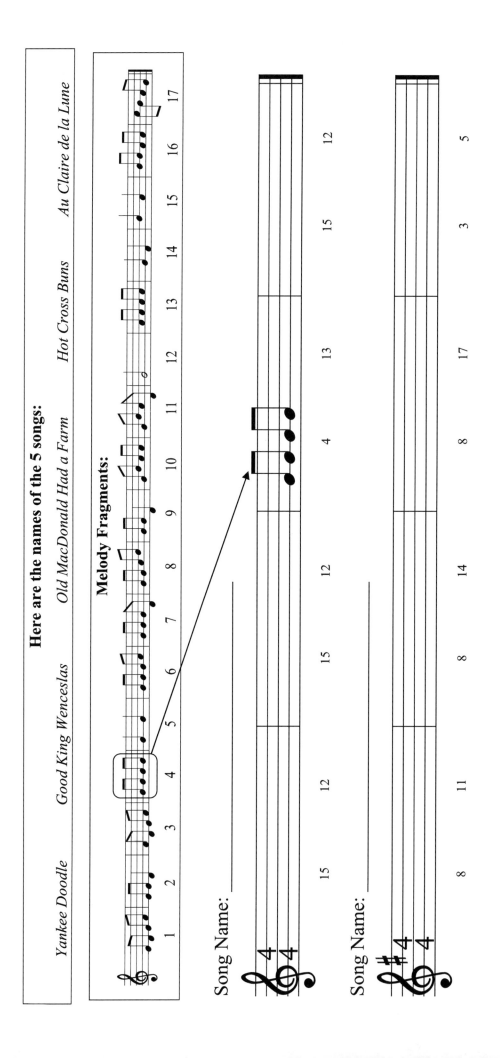

18

Name _____ Date _____ Classroom Teacher _____

Melody Fragments #1 - Page 2

Here are the names of the 5 songs:

Yankee Doodle *Good King Wenceslas* *Old MacDonald Had a Farm* *Hot Cross Buns* *Au Claire de la Lune*

Melody Fragments:

1 2 3 4 5 6 7 8 9 10 11 12 13 14 15 16 17

Song Name: _____

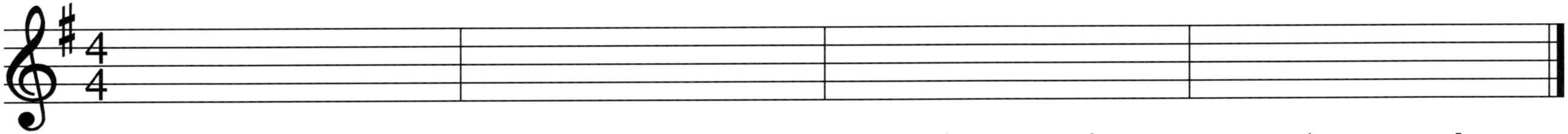

6   9   1   5

Song Name: _____

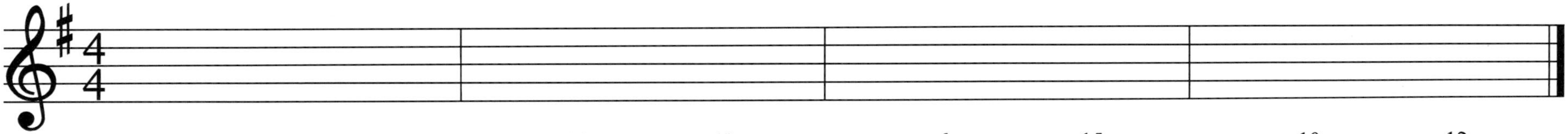

6   15   10   12   6   15   10   12

Song Name: _____

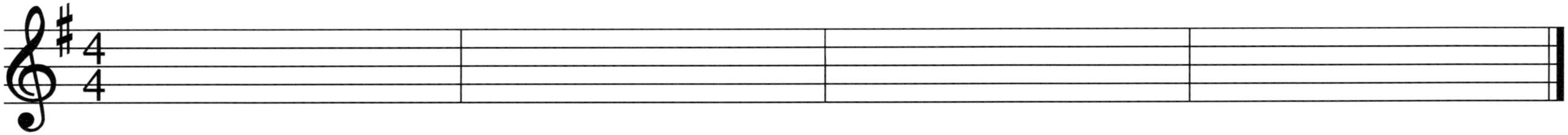

7   2   16   12   7   2   16   12

Name _____ Date _____ Classroom Teacher _____

Melody Fragments #2

Directions: Below are 17 melody fragments from 4 different songs. Match the melody fragments to the appropriate measures below. Neatly write the notes in the measure. One example has been done for you. Can you figure out the names of the songs? How many of these songs can you play on the xylophone or recorder?

Here are the names of the 4 songs:

London Bridges   *Ode to Joy*   *Ring Around the Rosy*   *Frère Jacques*

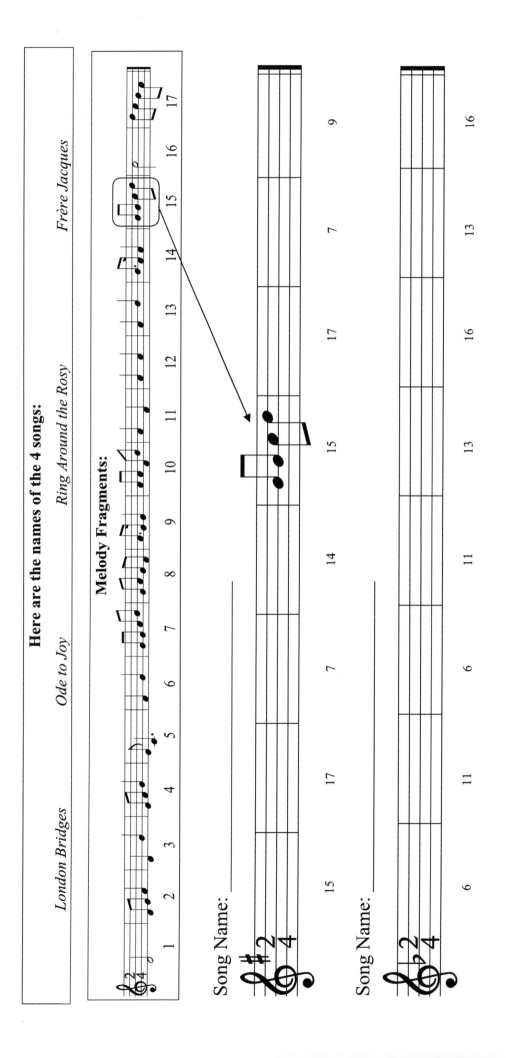

Melody Fragments #2 - Page 2

Name _____ Date _____ Classroom Teacher _____

Here are the names of the 4 songs:

London Bridges *Ode to Joy* *Ring Around the Rosy* *Frère Jacques*

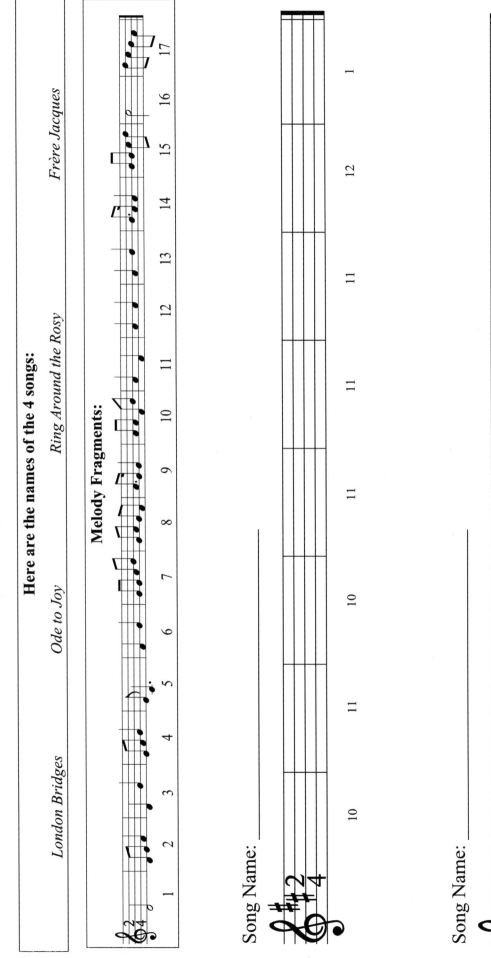

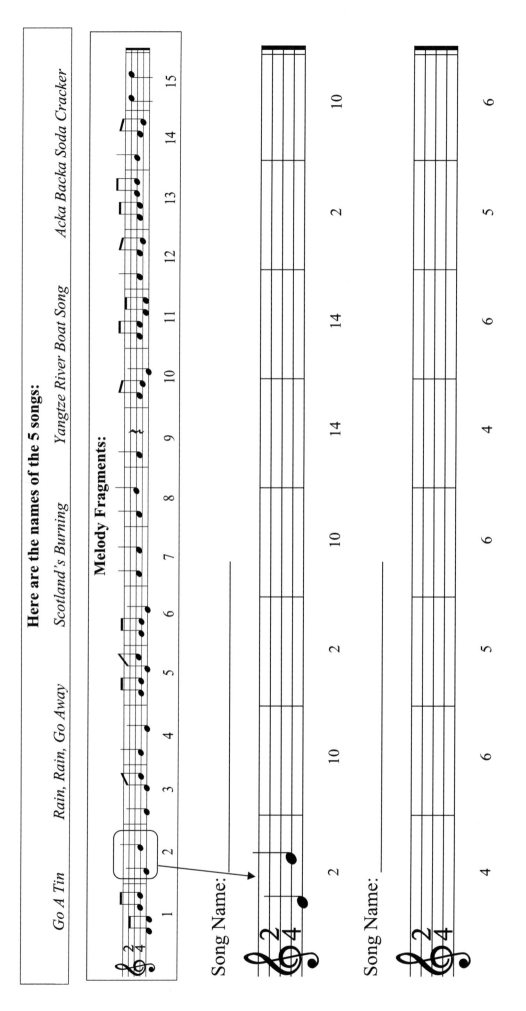

Name _____ Date _____ Classroom Teacher _____

Picture Rhythms #1

Directions: Circle the rhythm on the right that matches the picture rhythm on the left. Then, at the bottom of the page, fill in the blanks using the letters you circled. It will spell out two of the pictures on this page. Finally, clap the picture rhythms!

1.

2.

3.

4.

5.

6.

7.

8.

___ ___ ___ ___ ___   ___ ___ ___ ___
 1   2   3   4   5   6   7   8   8

Name _____ Date _____ Classroom Teacher _____

Picture Rhythms #2

Directions: Circle the rhythm on the right that matches the picture rhythm on the left. Then, at the bottom of the page, fill in the blanks using the letters you circled. It will spell out two of the pictures on this page. Finally, clap the picture rhythms!

	C	M	S
1.			
	A	O	T
2.			
	T	P	O
3.			
	N	D	T
4.			
	F	O	R
5.			
	O	G	I
6.			
	S	I	P
7.			
	O	H	U
8.			

___ ___ ___ ___   ___ ___ ___ ___
 1   2   3   4   5   6   7   8

© 2010 Heritage Music Press, a Lorenz company. All rights reserved.
This page may be reproduced for single-classroom use. This is a non-transferable license.

Name _____ Date _____ Classroom Teacher _____

Picture Rhythms #3

Directions: Circle the rhythm on the right that matches the picture rhythm on the left. Then, at the bottom of the page, fill in the blanks using the letters you circled. Be sure to match the letters to the correct blank. It will spell out two of the pictures on this page. Finally, clap the picture rhythms!

1.    S ♩ ♩ ♩ 𝄽   E ♩ 𝄽 ♩ 𝄽   T ♩ ♩ ♫ 𝄽

2.    A ♩ ♫ 𝄽 ♩   R ♩ ♫ ♩ 𝄽   O ♩ ♩ ♩ 𝄽

3.    R ♩ ♩ 𝄽 ♩   P ♩ ♩ ♩ ♩   E ♩ ♫ 𝄽

4.    P ♩ ♩ 𝄽 ♩   D ♩ 𝄽 ♩ 𝄽   O ♩ ♫ ♫

5.    I ♩ 𝄽 ♩ ♩   F ♩ 𝄽 ♩ 𝄽   G ♩ ♩ ♫

6.    H ♩ ♩ ♩ ♩   U ♩ 𝄽 ♫ ♫   T ♫ ♩ 𝄽

7. 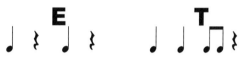   J ♩ ♩ ♩   A ♩ ♫ 𝄽   R ♩ ♩ ♫

8.    G ♩ 𝄽 ♫ 𝄽   K ♩ ♩ 𝄽   E ♩ ♫ ♫

___ ___ ___ ___
5   2   4   8

___ ___ ___ ___
1   6   7   3

© 2010 Heritage Music Press, a Lorenz company. All rights reserved.
This page may be reproduced for single-classroom use. This is a non-transferable license.

Rhythm Math #1

Directions: Add the note values for each example below. Instead of using a number, draw the type of note that has that value in the answer box. The notes, with their values, are in the box below. Number 1 is done for you.

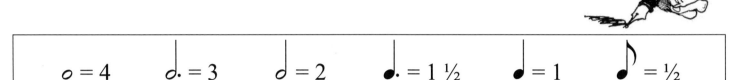

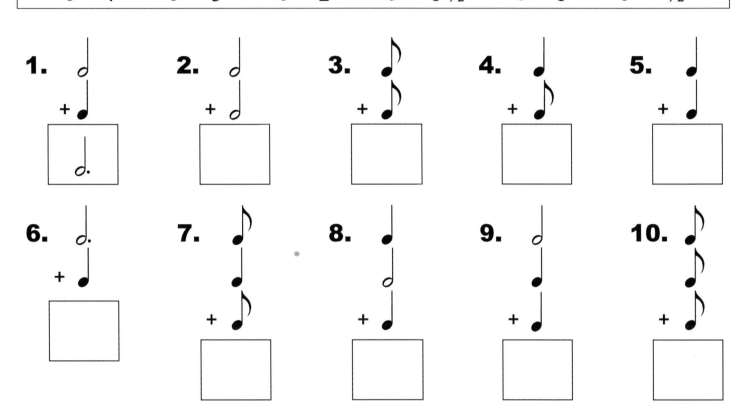

Directions: In music, a tie (curved line from one note to another) is used to tell the musician to add the notes together and play/sing the notes as one longer note. Write the note in the blank that adds up to the total of the notes being tied together. Number 11 is done for you.

11. ♩‿♩ = ♩ (half note)

12. ♩‿♩ = ___

13. ♪‿♪ = ___

14. ♪‿♪‿♪ = ___

15. ♩‿♩ = ___

16. ♪‿♩ = ___

17. ♪‿♪‿♪‿♪ = ___

18. ♩‿♪‿♪‿♪ = ___

© 2010 Heritage Music Press, a Lorenz company. All rights reserved.
This page may be reproduced for single-classroom use. This is a non-transferable license.

Name _____ Date _____ Classroom Teacher _____

Rhythm Math #2

Directions: Add the note and rest values for each example below. Instead of using a number, draw the type of note that has that value in the answer box. The notes and rests, with their values, are in the box below. Number 1 is done for you.

| $o = 4$ | $\mathrm{d.} = 3$ | $\mathrm{d} = 2$ | $\mathrm{d.} = 1\frac{1}{2}$ | $\mathrm{d} = 1$ | $\mathrm{\flat} = \frac{1}{2}$ |
| — = 4 | —. = 3 | — = 2 | $\{ = 1\frac{1}{2}$ | $\{ = 1$ | $\mathrm{\gamma} = \frac{1}{2}$ |

1. ♪ + ₹. = 𝅗𝅥
2. ♩. + ♪ =
3. ▬. + ♩ =
4. 𝄽 + ♩ =
5. ♩ + ♩ =

6. ♪ + 𝄽 =
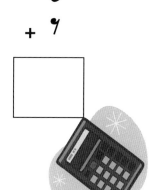

7. 𝄽 + 𝅗𝅥 + ♪ =

8. ♩. + 𝄽 + ♪ =

9. ♩ + 𝄽 + 𝄽. + ♪ =

10. 𝄽 + ♪ + 𝄽 + ♪ =

Directions: In music, a tie (curved line from one note to another) is used to tell the musician to add the notes together and play/sing the notes as one longer note. Write a combination of notes (only one note per box) that adds up to the note given. There may be more than one correct answer.

11. o = ☐‿☐‿☐‿☐   13. ♩. = ☐‿☐

12. 𝅗𝅥 = ☐‿☐‿☐   14. ♩. = ☐‿☐‿☐

© 2010 Heritage Music Press, a Lorenz company. All rights reserved.
This page may be reproduced for single-classroom use. This is a non-transferable license.

Name _____ Date _____ Classroom Teacher _____

Rhythm Math #3

Directions: Add or subtract the note and rest values for each example below. Instead of using a number, draw the type of note or rest that has that value in the answer box. Each answer box indicates if you should draw a note or a rest. The notes and rests, with their values, are in the box below.

$o = 4$	$d. = 3$	$d = 2$	$\bullet. = 1\frac{1}{2}$	$\bullet = 1$	$\flat = \frac{1}{2}$	$\flat = \frac{1}{4}$
▬ = 4	▬. = 3	▬ = 2	ξ. = 1½	ξ = 1	ɣ = ½	ɣ = ¼

1. ♩ + ▬ = ☐ rest

2. o − d. = ☐ note

3. ♪ + ♬ = ☐ rest

4. ξ. − ♪ = ☐ note

5. ♩. + ξ. = ☐ rest

6. o − d = ☐ note

7. ♪ + ξ = ☐ rest (+ ♪)

8. ɣ + d + ♪ + ξ = ☐ note

9. ▬ + ♪ + ♩ + ♪ = ☐ rest

10. ♪ + ɣ + ♪ + ɣ = ☐ note

Directions: In music, a tie (curved line from one note to another) is used to tell the musician to add the notes together and play/sing the notes as one longer note. Write a combination of notes (only one note per box) that adds up to the note given. There may be more than one correct answer.

11. d = ☐ ☐ ☐ ☐

12. $\bullet.$ = ☐ ☐ ☐

13. o = ☐ ☐

14. $\bullet$ = ☐ ☐ ☐ ☐

© 2010 Heritage Music Press, a Lorenz company. All rights reserved.
This page may be reproduced for single-classroom use. This is a non-transferable license.

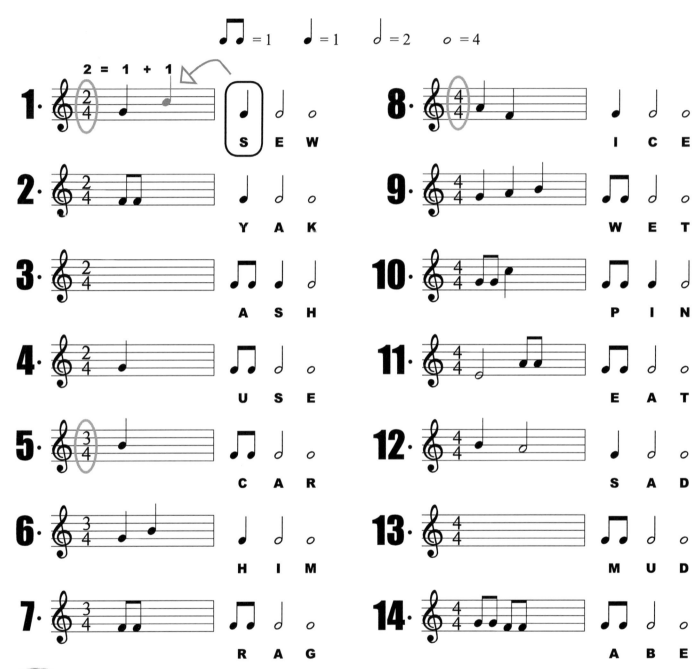

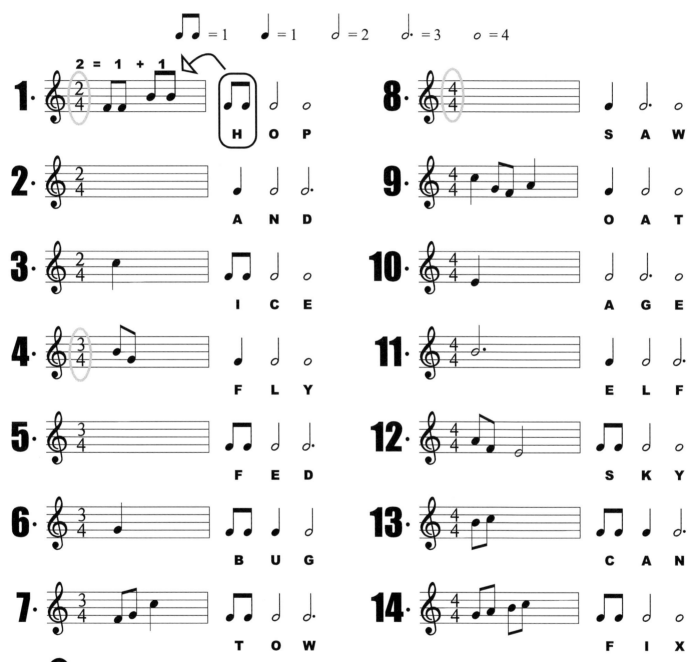

Name _____ Date _____ Classroom Teacher _____

Case of the Missing Notes #3

Directions: Each of the measures below are incomplete. Based on the time signature (2/4, 3/4 or 4/4) circle the rhythm figure that will complete the measure and draw it at the end of the measure. You may draw it on any line or space you chose. Remember that the top number in the time signature tells you how many beats (not notes) are in each measure. Here's a list of note values for this exercise:

♪ = ½   ♫ = 1   ♩ = 1   ♩. = 1½   𝅗𝅥 = 2   𝅗𝅥. = 3   o = 4

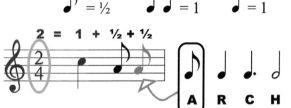

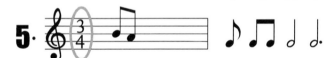

When you're finished, write the letter shown under the note you circled in the blank that matches the question number. Number 1 has been for you.

What do you do if you can't find a rubber band?

__ __ __ __   __   __ __ __ __ __ __   __ __ __ __ __ __ __ __ A
13 4 12 5   7   8 15 9 11 3 4 10   6 16 10 14 2 11 3 16 1

© 2010 Heritage Music Press, a Lorenz company. All rights reserved.
This page may be reproduced for single-classroom use. This is a non-transferable license.

Case of the Missing Notes #5

Directions: Each of the measures below are incomplete. Based on the time signature ($\frac{2}{4}$, $\frac{3}{4}$, $\frac{4}{4}$ or $\frac{6}{8}$) circle the rhythmic figure that will complete the measure and draw it at the end of the measure. You may draw it on any line or space you chose. Remember that the top number in the time signature tells you how many beats (not notes) are in each measure.

When you're finished, write the letter shown under the note you circled in the blank that matches the question number. Number 1 has been for you.

How do you do make a bandstand?

T _ _ _ _ _ _ _ _ _ _ _ _ _ _ _ !
1 14 3 6   2 8 11 9   12 4 6 10 16   7 4 15 10 13 5

Name _____ Date _____ Classroom Teacher _____

Rhythm Logic #1

Directions: Fill in the empty boxes with notes—only one note per box. The rhythmic sum of each row is shown at the right and the sum of each column is at the bottom. Some puzzles have been started for you. There may be more than one correct solution to each puzzle grid. Here are the notes and rests you can use and their rhythmic values.

♪ = ½   ♩ = 1   ♩. = 1½   𝅗𝅥 = 2   𝅗𝅥. = 3   𝅝 = 4

❶
𝅝		5
		2½
4½	3	

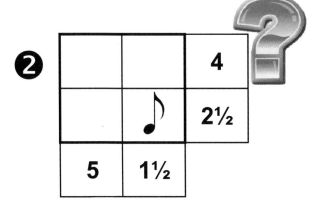

❷
		4
	♪	2½
5	1½	

❸
	𝅗𝅥	4
		7
6	5	

❹
		4½
		2
2	4½	

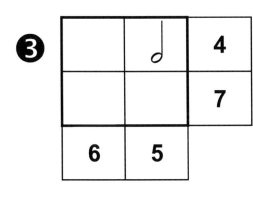

❺
			3
	♩.		4½
		♪	6½
4½	8	1½	

❻
♪			3½
			6½
		𝅝	7
5½	6	5½	

Name _____ Date _____ Classroom Teacher _____

Rhythm Logic #2

Directions: Fill in the empty boxes with notes or rests–only one per box. Use at least one note and one rest in each puzzle. The rhythmic sum of each row is shown at the right and the sum of each column at the bottom. Some puzzles have been started for you. There may be more than one correct solution to each puzzle grid. Here are the notes and rests you can use and their rhythmic values.

♪ = ½   ♩ = 1   ♩. = 1½   ♩ = 2   ♩. = 3   o = 4

𝄾 = ½   𝄽 = 1   𝄽 = 1½   ▬ = 2   ▬. = 3   ▬ = 4

1.

𝄽		3
		3½
4	2½	

2.

		5½
	♪	1½
2½	4½	

3.

		4
		2
3½	2½	

4.

		6
		1
4½	2½	

5.

			5½
𝄽			3½
		𝄾	7½
5½	7	4	

6.

			12
			5
			6
8½	8	6½	

36   © 2010 Heritage Music Press, a Lorenz company. All rights reserved.
This page may be reproduced for single-classroom use. This is a non-transferable license.

Name _____ Date _____ Classroom Teacher _____

Rhythm Logic #3

Directions: Fill in the empty boxes with notes or rests—only one per box. Use at least one note and one rest in each puzzle. The rhythmic sum of each row is shown at the right and the sum of each column at the bottom. Some puzzles have been started for you. There may be more than one correct solution to each puzzle grid. Here are the notes and rests you can use and their rhythmic values.

♬ = ¼   ♪ = ½   ♩ = 1   ♩. = 1½   𝅗𝅥 = 2   𝅗𝅥. = 3   o = 4

𝄽 = ¼   𝄽 = ½   𝄽 = 1   𝄽. = 1½   𝄽 = 2   𝄽. = 3   𝄽 = 4

❶

♪		1¼
		2½
2¼	1½	

❷

		¾
		5½
2	4¼	

❸

			2½
			6½
			5½
2¼	9	3¼	

❹

				1
				6½
		𝄽		5
				7¼
4½	6¾	2¾	5¾	

❺

				9¼
				4¼
				4¾
				5¼
4¾	4	7½	7¼	

Name _____ Date _____ Classroom Teacher _____

Mystery Rhythms #1

Directions: Use the clues below each measure to figure out what notes you should write in that measure. Remember to look at the time signature for each problem. The top number of the time signature tells you how many beats (not notes) should go in each measure. In other words, all the notes in each measure need to add up to the top number of the time signature.

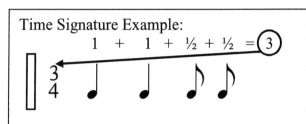

You may use these note values only:

♪ = ½   ♩ = 1   ♩ = 2   o = 4

You may beam 2 eighth notes together, such as ♪♪ = ♫

① 2/4

    2 of the same kind of note   4 of the same kind of note   2 of one kind of note and 1 of another kind; put the longer note first   1 note

② 3/4

    2 of one kind of note 2 of another kind of note; put the longer notes first   2 notes of different length, shorter one last   2 of one kind of note and 1 of another kind; put the longer note last

③ 3/4

    4 of one kind of note and 1 of another kind; put the long note in the middle   3 of the same kind of note   2 of one kind of note and 1 of another kind; put the longer note first

④ 4/4

    4 of the same kind of note   4 of one kind of note and 2 of another kind, put the shorter ones in the middle   2 of one kind of note and 1 of another kind; put the longer note first   1 note

⑤ 4/4

    5 notes; put the long note first; 4 notes are the same value   4 notes; only 2 can be the same kind of note; write them from long to short   3 notes; shorter notes first   2 notes

© 2010 Heritage Music Press, a Lorenz company. All rights reserved.
This page may be reproduced for single-classroom use. This is a non-transferable license.

Name _____ Date _____ Classroom Teacher _____

Mystery Rhythms #2

Directions: Use the clues below each measure to figure out what notes you should write in that measure. Remember to look at the time signature for each problem. The top number of the time signature tells you how many beats (not notes) should go in each measure. In other words, all the notes in each measure need to add up to the top number of the time signature. Some measures may have more than one correct answer.

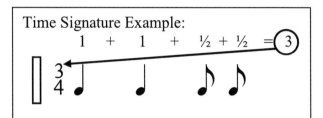

You may use these note values only:

♪ = ½   ♩ = 1   ♩. = 1½   𝅗𝅥 = 2   𝅗𝅥. = 3   𝅝 = 4

You may beam 2 eighth notes together, such as ♪♪ = ♫

❶ 2/4

| 1 note | 2 of the same kind of note | 2 notes of different lengths; put the longer one first | 2 shorter notes on either side of a longer note |

❷ 3/4

| 3 of the same kind of note | 4 notes; put the shorter notes in the middle | 1 note | 2 notes; put the longer note first |

❸ 4/4

| 6 notes in this pattern short-short-long-short-short-long | 4 of the same kind of note | 2 notes of different lengths | 1 note |

❹ 4/4

| 2 of the same kind of note | 8 notes; all the same length | 3 notes; 2 of one kind and 1 of another; put the shortest note last | 3 notes of different lengths; put the longest one first and the shortest one last |

❺ 4/4

| 2 notes of one kind and 2 of another; long-short-long-short | 4 notes of 3 different kinds; put them in an alternating shorter-longer pattern put the longest one last | 6 notes; put the shortest ones in the middle | 1 longer note in between 2 of the same kind of shorter notes |

© 2010 Heritage Music Press, a Lorenz company. All rights reserved.
This page may be reproduced for single-classroom use. This is a non-transferable license.

Name _____ Date _____ Classroom Teacher _____

Mystery Rhythms #3

Directions: Use the clues below each measure to figure out what notes you should write in that measure. Remember to look at the time signature for each problem. The top number of the time signature tells you how many beats (not notes) should go in each measure. In other words, all the notes in each measure need to add up to the top number of the time signature. Some measures may have more than one correct answer.

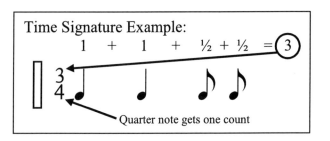

You may use these note values only:

$\eighth = ¼$ $\quarter = ½$ $\quarter = 1$ $\quarter. = 1½$
$\half = 2$ $\half. = 3$ $\whole = 4$

You may beam 2 eighth notes together (♪♪ = ♫),
and 4 sixteenth notes (♬♬♬♬ = ▦),
and 1 eighth / 2 sixteenth notes (♪♬♬ = ♫♬).

❶ ‖ 2/4 | | | | ‖

     2 notes of different lengths;   8 of the same   1 note   3 notes;
     put the short one first   kind of note   put the longest one in the middle

❷ ‖ 3/4 | | | | ‖

   3 of the same   2 of the same   2 of one kind of note and   6 of the same
   kind of note   kind of note   4 of another kind of note;   kind of note
                                               put the longer notes first and last

❸ ‖ 4/4 | | | | ‖

 4 of one kind of note and   2 of one kind of note and   2 notes of one kind and   3 different lengths of notes;
 3 of another kind of note;   2 of another kind of note;   1 of another kind of note;   put them in order from
 put the shorter notes first   put them in   put the longest one first   shortest to longest
                      long-short-long-short order

❹ ‖ 4/4 | | | | ‖

 4 notes of 2 different lengths;   16 notes   4 of the shortest kind of note   13 notes total;
 put the long ones first   and 1 longer note;   12 are the same length
                                                put the long note in the middle   put the longest note last

❺ ‖ 4/4 | | | | ‖

 4 of the same   10 notes of 2 different kinds;   9 notes of 3 different lengths;   4 sets of notes that have a
 kind of note   put them in   put them in order from   long-short-short pattern;
                short-short-short-short-long,   longest to shortest   12 notes in total
                short-short-short-short-long order

© 2010 Heritage Music Press, a Lorenz company. All rights reserved.
This page may be reproduced for single-classroom use. This is a non-transferable license.

Name _____ Date _____ Classroom Teacher _____

Transforming Rhythms #1

Directions: Change the rhythm of the song in step 1 (*Hot Cross Buns*) to another song's rhythm. Rewrite each line of rhythms by following the directions in each step. Step 2 has been started for you. Clap and say each line when you are done.

1. Start with rhythm in the song *Hot Cross Buns*.

2. Reverse the order of notes in each measure.

3. Replace every half note with 4 eighth notes.

4. Replace the 1st quarter note in the 1st measure to 2 eighth notes.

5. Combine the last 2 notes in the 4th measure into 1 note.

6. In the 2nd measure, switch the 2nd set of eighth notes with the 1st quarter note.

What song has *Hot Cross Buns* transformed into?

_____

(Here are some options: *Jingle Bells, Au Claire de la Lune, Mary Mack, Mary Had a Little Lamb, Happy Birthday,* or *Yangtze River.*)

© 2010 Heritage Music Press, a Lorenz company. All rights reserved.
This page may be reproduced for single-classroom use. This is a non-transferable license.

Name _____ Date _____ Classroom Teacher _____

Transforming Rhythms #2

Directions: Change the rhythm of the song in step 1 (*Jingle Bells*) to another song's rhythm. Rewrite each line of rhythms by following the directions in each step. Clap and say each line when you are done.

1. Start with rhythm from the first 4 measures of the song *Jingle Bells*…

2. Switch measure 1 and 2.

3. Reverse the rhythm in measure 4.

4. Replace the half note with 2 eighth notes and 1 quarter note, in that order.

5. Replace the last 3 eighth notes of the song with a dotted quarter note. Combine the last 3 notes in the 3rd measure into 1 note.

6. Replace the 1st and 6th set of beamed eighth notes to a dotted eighth and sixteenth note combination (♪♪).

What song has *Jingle Bells* transformed into?

_____

(Here are some options: *Hot Cross Buns, London Bridges, Mary Mack, Mary Had a Little Lamb, Happy Birthday,* or *This Old Man.*)

© 2010 Heritage Music Press, a Lorenz company. All rights reserved.
This page may be reproduced for single-classroom use. This is a non-transferable license.

Name _____ Date _____ Classroom Teacher _____

Transforming Rhythms #3

Directions: Change the rhythm of the song in step 1 (*Au Claire de la Lune*) to another song's rhythm. Rewrite each line of rhythms by following the directions in each step. Clap and say each line when you are done.

1. Start with the rhythm from the first 4 measures of the song *Au Claire de la Lune*…

2. Switch beat 2 and 3 in the 1st measure.

3. Rewrite all half notes to 2 eighth notes and a quarter note.

4. Replace the 3rd quarter note of the song with a 1 eighth note and 2 sixteenth note combination (♪𝅘𝅥𝅯𝅘𝅥𝅯).

5. Replace the 3rd beat in the 3rd measure with 4 sixteenth notes.

6. Replace the 7th set of 2 eighth notes of the song with a 2 sixteenth note and 1 eighth note combination (𝅘𝅥𝅯𝅘𝅥𝅯♪).

What song has *Au Claire de la Lune* transformed into?

_____

(Here are some options: *Hot Cross Buns, London Bridges, Mary Mack, Mary Had a Little Lamb, Old MacDonald,* or *This Old Man*.)

© 2010 Heritage Music Press, a Lorenz company. All rights reserved.
This page may be reproduced for single-classroom use. This is a non-transferable license.

Name _____ Date _____ Classroom Teacher _____

Meter Matching #1

Directions: Each letter has a one-measure rhythmic fragment next to it. Match the rhythms with their corresponding time signatures by filling in the letter next to each time signature. The first one has been done for you. Each set of time signatures should spell a word, which is part of a short sentence.

Some things to remember:

Top number   4 = number of beats in measure (**4**)   ♪ = ½   ♩♪ = 1   ♬ = 1

Bottom number 4 = note value that gets one beat (♩)   ♩ = 1   𝅗𝅥 = 2   o = 4

2/4 **S**
3/4 ___
4/4 ___
5/4 ___

3/4 ___

2/4 ___
3/4 ___
4/4 ___

2/4 ___
3/4 ___
4/4 ___
5/4 ___

2/4 ___
3/4 ___
4/4 ___
5/4 ___
6/4 ___

T ♪♪♪
G ♩ ♩ ♩ ♩
I ♫ ♫ ♫
D ♫ ♩ 𝅗𝅥 ♩

I o

W ♩ ♫ ♩
I ♩ ♫ ♪
N ♬ ♩

N 𝅗𝅥 𝅗𝅥
O ♩ ♫ ♩
B 𝅗𝅥 𝅗𝅥 ♫ ♩
A ♬

A ♫.
D ♩ ♫ ♫ ♩
O ♩ ♩
R ♩
E ♪♩ ♫ ♪

S ♩ ♩
A 𝅗𝅥 ♫ ♩ ♩ ♩
N ♫ ♩ ♫ ♩
E 𝅗𝅥 o

A ♩ ♫ ♩

E ♫ ♬
A 𝅗𝅥 𝅗𝅥 𝅗𝅥
T ♩ ♫ ♫

S ♫ ♬
L o ♫
U ♪♪♪
G ♩ ♩ ♫

U ♬
T ♬ ♬
I ♪
X ♫ ♩ ♩
Y ♩ 𝅗𝅥 ♩

44

Meter Matching #2

Directions: Each letter has a one-measure rhythmic fragment next to it. Match the rhythms with their corresponding time signatures by filling in the letter next to each time signature. The first one has been done for you. Each set of time signatures should spell a word, which is part of a short sentence.

Some things to remember:

Top number **3** = number of beats in measure
Bottom number **4** = note value that gets one beat

♪ = ¼   ♪ = ½   ♪. = ¾   ♫ = 1   ♬ = 1
♩ = 1   ♩. = 1½   𝅗𝅥 = 2   𝅗𝅥. = 3   o = 4

2/4 __Y__
3/4 ___
4/4 ___

O ♩ ♫ ♬
M ♩ ♩ ♫ ♩ ♩
B ♬ ♩ ♩ ♩

Y ♬ ♬
A ♩ ♪ ♩ ♪ ♪
U 𝅗𝅥 ♪ ♩ ♪♪

3/4 ___
4/4 ___
5/4 ___

S ♩. ♩ ♩ ♪
A ♩ ♫ ♬
E ♪ o ♪

R 𝅗𝅥. ♬
U ♪ ♪ ♪♪
N ♩ ♩ ♫ ♩ ♩. ♪

2/4 ___
3/4 ___
4/4 ___
6/4 ___

E ♬ ♬ ♩
R ♫ ♫ ♫
A 𝅗𝅥. 𝅗𝅥. ♩ ♪
N ♩ ♪ ♩ ♪

M ♪ ♪ ♪ ♪ ♪
Y 𝅗𝅥. ♩. ♪ ♩
V ♪ ♩ ♪
O ♩. o ♪

2/4 ___
3/4 ___
4/4 ___
5/4 ___
6/4 ___

Q ♬ ♪ ♬
A ♬ ♫ ♩. ♪
B o ♩ ♩
E ♪ ♪ ♪ ♪ ♪
T o ♩

L ♫ ♬ ♪ ♫
R ♩ ♪ ♩ ♪ ♩
M ♩ ♪ ♩ ♪ ♩ ♪
U ♩. ♩ ♩ ♩
S ♪ ♬ ♪

Name _____ Date _____ Classroom Teacher _____

Meter Matching #3

Directions: Each letter has a one-measure rhythmic fragment next to it. Match the rhythms with their corresponding time signatures by filling in the letter next to each time signature. The first one has been done for you. Each set of time signatures should spell a word, which is part of a short sentence.

Some things to remember:

Top number   6 = number of beats in measure (**6**)

Bottom number   8 = note value that gets one beat (♪)

2/4 ____
3/4 ____
4/4 ____

Y ♩ ♩. ♪
A ♬♬ ♩
M ♪ ♩

S ♬♬♩ ♬♬♪♪
O ♩ ♪♪
W ♩ ♩

4/4 ____
6/8 ____

F ♬♩. ♬♩.
O ♬♬

T ♩ ♬ ♬♩
A ♪♪♪

3/4 ____
4/4 ____

S ♬♬ ♬
E ♩ ♪ ♪♩.

O ♩. ♪♩
G ♩.

6/8 ____
9/8 ____

M ♩ ♪ ♪
I ♬ ♩.

Y ♬♬♩.
A ♩ ♬♩ ♪

2/4 ____
3/4 ____
4/4 ____
3/8 ____
9/8 ____
12/8 ____

N ♩ ♪♬♩.
C ♩ ♬♩
I ♬♩.
K ♪♪♪♪♪
L ♬♬♬♬
E ♪♪♪

R ♩ ♬♩
A ♬♩ ♬♪
P ♩ ♪♩
F ♩. ♪
D ♬♩ ♪♬♩
U ♪♩.

© 2010 Heritage Music Press, a Lorenz company. All rights reserved.
This page may be reproduced for single-classroom use. This is a non-transferable license.

Name _____   Date _____   Classroom Teacher _____

Rhythigram #1: *Hot Cross Buns*

Directions: These are musical Tangrams. The object of the puzzle is to put the Rhythigram together so that is it the rhythm of the indicated song. Follow these steps and tips to complete the puzzle:

1. Cut out all the pieces and turn them so that the notes are oriented the correct way.
2. There may be several ways the puzzle pieces fit together, but only one way will result in the song's correct rhythm.
3. The final puzzle should be a 4X4 grid (16 beats, 4 measure in $\frac{4}{4}$ time.)
4. The first note in this song's rhythm is a quarter note.
5. When you are finished, clap the rhythm to check your work.

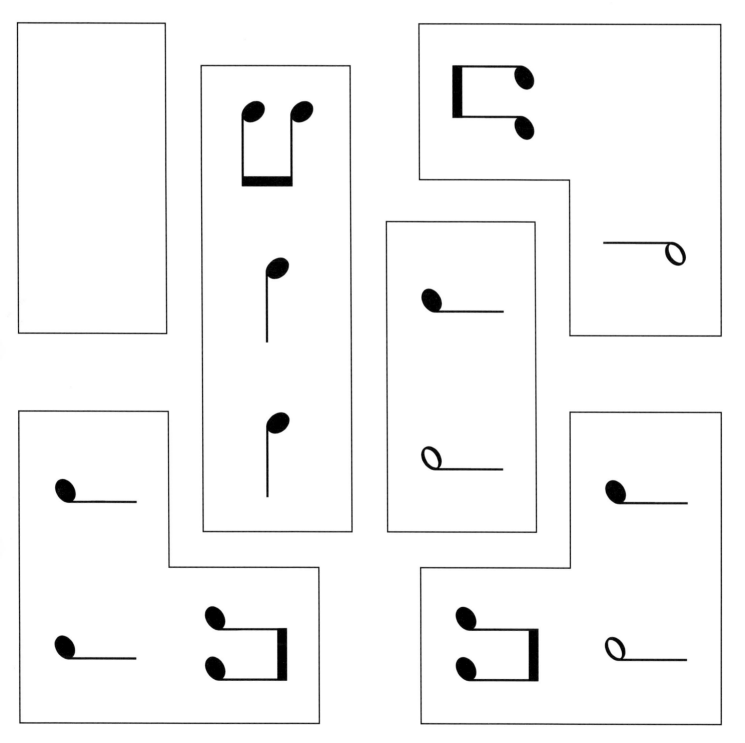

© 2010 Heritage Music Press, a Lorenz company. All rights reserved.
This page may be reproduced for single-classroom use. This is a non-transferable license.

Name _____ Date _____ Classroom Teacher _____

Rhythigram #2: *Jingle Bells*

Directions: These are musical Tangrams. The object of the puzzle is to put the Rhythigram together so that is it the rhythm of the indicated song. Follow these steps and tips to complete the puzzle:

1. Cut out all the pieces and turn them so that the notes are oriented the correct way.
2. There may be several ways the puzzle pieces fit together, but only one way will result in the song's correct rhythm.
3. The final puzzle should be a 4X4 grid (16 beats, 4 measure in $\frac{4}{4}$ time.)
4. The first note in this song's rhythm is a pair of beamed eighth-notes.
5. When you are finished, clap the rhythm to check your work.

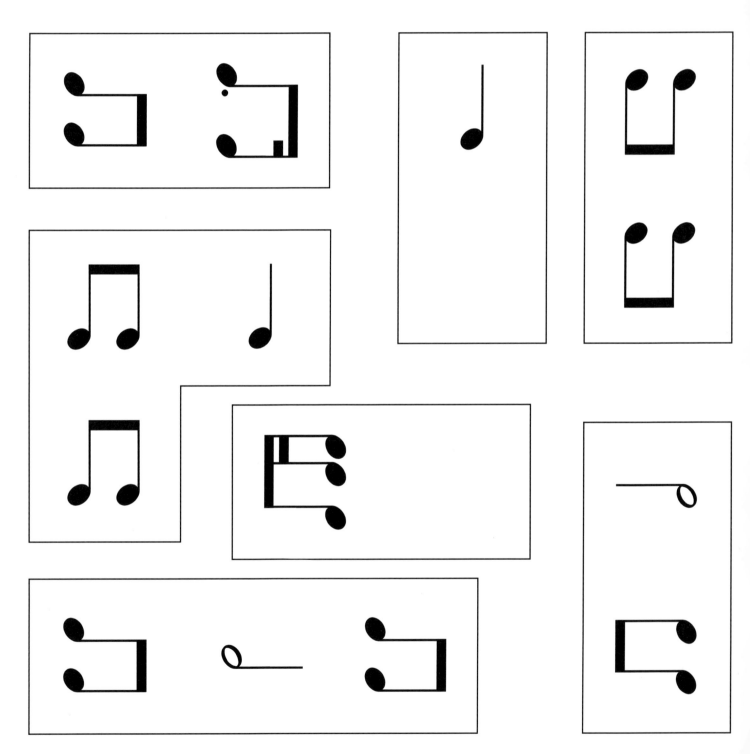

48

© 2010 Heritage Music Press, a Lorenz company. All rights reserved.
This page may be reproduced for single-classroom use. This is a non-transferable license.

Name _____ Date _____ Classroom Teacher _____

Rhythigram #3: *Mary Had a Little Lamb*

Directions: These are musical Tangrams. The object of the puzzle is to put the Rhythigram together so that is it the rhythm of the indicated song. Follow these steps and tips to complete the puzzle:

1. Cut out all the pieces and turn them so that the notes are oriented the correct way.
2. There may be several ways the puzzle pieces fit together, but only one way will result in the song's correct rhythm.
3. The final puzzle should be a 4X4 grid (16 beats, 4 measure in $\frac{4}{4}$ time.)
4. The first note in this song's rhythm is a pair of beamed eighth-notes.
5. When you are finished, clap the rhythm to check your work.

© 2010 Heritage Music Press, a Lorenz company. All rights reserved.
This page may be reproduced for single-classroom use. This is a non-transferable license.

Answer Key

Note Name Words #1, page 3
1. Cow
2. Rat
3. Dog
4. Bat
5. Bird
6. Bear
7. Bee
8. Panda
9. Camel
10. Eagle

Note Name Words #2, page 4
1. Soda
2. Pear
3. Cake
4. Bean
5. Egg
6. Grape
7. Bacon
8. Peach
9. Beef
10. Bagel

Note Name Words #3, page 5
1. Dart
2. Car
3. Dice
4. Game
5. Cards
6. Bicycle
7. Barbie™
8. Frisbee®
9. Bubbles
10. Candy Land™

Note Name Phrases #1, page 6
1. A beige giraffe dodged a fast cat.
2. The amoeba grabbed a black waffle.
3. The bearded beggar ate a bagel.
4. An eager dude attended Baghdad Academy.
5. The egg-headed idea was defeated.
6. The geese danced to the reggae beat.

Note Name Phrases #2, page 7
1. The dog ran away and evaded capture.
2. The damaged baggage went to Canada.
3. The algae cascaded over the bridge.
4. He found a dagger in the garbage.
5. They decoded a message with a gadget.
6. She decided to make a beanbag game.

Note Name Phrases #3, page 8
1. I feared a bad grade in algebra.
2. Dice and card games are really fun.
3. The façade of the arcade is big.
4. The cat crawled under the bread table.
5. The crabby mage baked a green cake.
6. She ate an egg and seaweed burger.

Reading Solfege #1, page 9
What kind of music do mummies listen to?
 Wrap music
What kind of music do Martians like?
 Nep-tunes

Reading Solfege #2, page 10
Why did Mozart get rid of his chickens?
 They kept saying "Bach, Bach!"

Reading Solfege #3, page 11
Why was the music teacher locked out of her classroom?
 She left her keys in the piano!

Melodic Direction #1, page 12

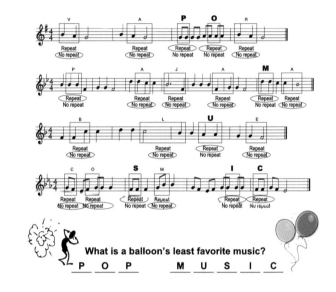

What is a balloon's least favorite music?
P O P   M U S I C

Melodic Direction #2, page 13

What food is essential for good music?
T H E   B E E T

Answer Key

Melodic direction #3, page 14

Going Up! Going Down! #1, page 15

Going Up! Going Down! #2, page 16

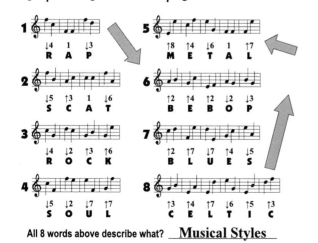

Going Up! Going Down! #3, page 17

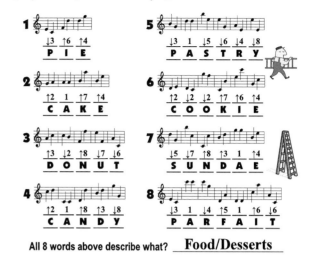

Melody Fragments #1, page 18

Melody Fragments #2, page 20

Answer Key

Melody Fragments #3, page 22

Picture Rhythms #1, page 24
1. H
2. O
3. U
4. S
5. E
6. B
7. A
8. L

    House   Ball

Picture Rhythms #2, page 25
1. M
2. O
3. O
4. N
5. F
6. I
7. S
8. H

    Moon   Fish

Picture Rhythms #3, page 26
1. S
2. R
3. R
4. O
5. F
6. T
7. A
8. G

    Frog   Star

Rhythm Math #1, page 27

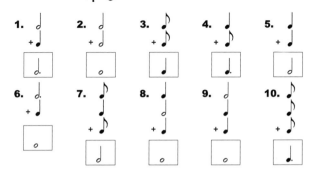

Rhythm Math #2, page 28

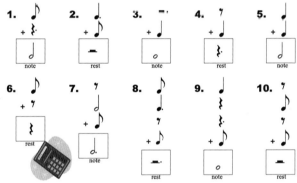

Rhythm Math #3, page 29

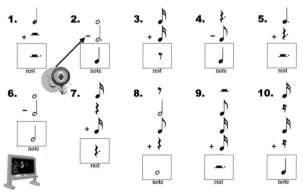

Answer Key

Case of the Missing Notes #1, page 30

Why couldn't Mozart find his teacher?
BECAUSE HE WAS HAYDN!

Case of the Missing Notes #2, page 31

What do trombone players like best at the playground?
GOING DOWN THE SLIDE!

Case of the Missing Notes #3, page 32

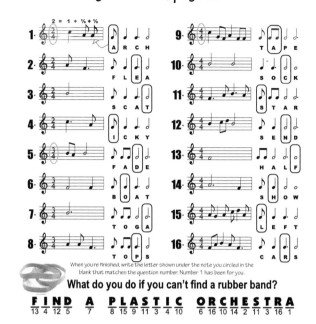

What do you do if you can't find a rubber band?
FIND A PLASTIC ORCHESTRA

Case of the Missing Notes #4, page 33

What kind of music do ghosts prefer?
SPIRITUALS, OF COURSE!

Answer Key

Case of the Missing Notes #5, page 34

Rhythm Logic #2, page 36

Rhythm Logic #1, page 35

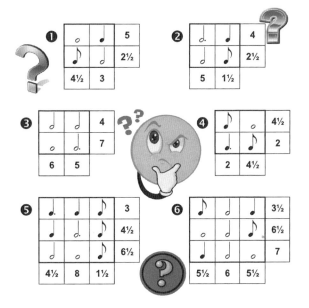

Rhythm Logic #3, page 37

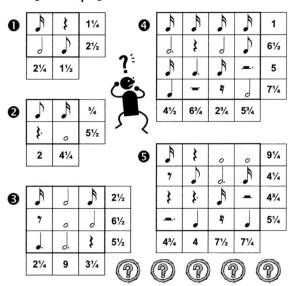

Mystery Rhythms #1, page 38

Answer Key

Mystery Rhythms #2, page 39

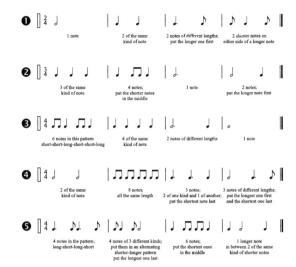

Mystery Rhythms #3, page 40

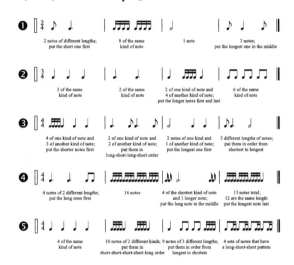

Transforming Rhythms #1, page 41

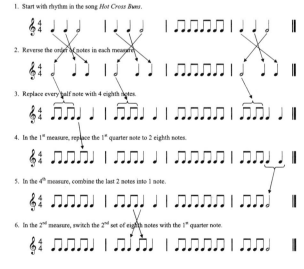

Transforming Rhythms #2, page 42

What song has *Jingle Bells* transformed into?
London Bridges

(Here are some options: *Hot Cross Buns, London Bridges, Mary Mack, Mary Had a Little Lamb, Happy Birthday,* or *This Old Man*)

Transforming Rhythms #3, page 43

What song has *Au Claire de la Lune* transformed into?
This Old Man

(Here are some options: *Hot Cross Buns, London Bridges, Mary Mack, Mary Had a Little Lamb, Old MacDonald,* or *This Old Man*)

Meter Matching #1, page 44
Sing a new song today.

Meter Matching #2, page 45
You are very smart.

Meter Matching #3, page 46
Way to go my friend.

Answer Key

Rhythigram #1, page 47

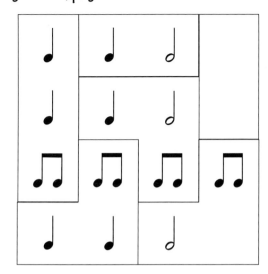

Rhythigram #3, page 49

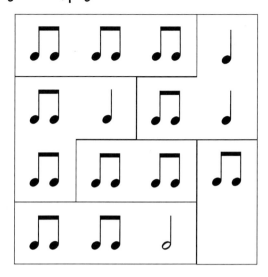

Rhythigram #2, page 48

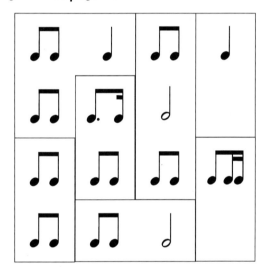